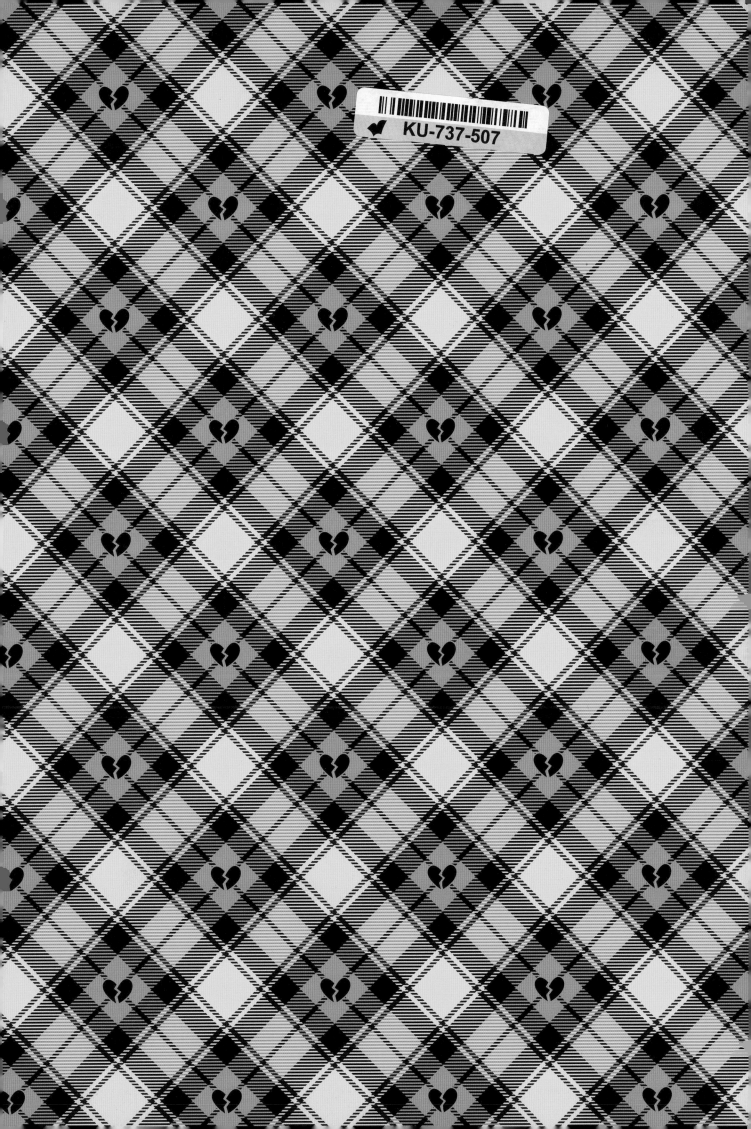

Published 2020. Little Brother Books Ltd, Ground Floor,
23 Southernhay East, Exeter, Devon, EX1 1QL
Printed In Poland.

books@littlebrotherbooks.co.uk | www.littlebrotherbooks.co.uk

lolsurprise.com | mgae.com

CONTENTS

TURN UP THE BRIGHT!

Bring your sunglasses, because this year we're bolder than ever! Channelling fashion, sass, music and class, there's some new L.O.L.s to meet.

GLITTER FILTER ON, LET'S DO THIS!

A LIL' ART HERE AND THERE.

DRIP DROP
CLUB: ART **RARITY:** ULTRA RARE

WANT ☐ OWN ☐

PROGRAMMED 4 THE DANCE FLOOR.

DANCEBOT
CLUB: DANCE **RARITY:** FABULOUS

WANT ☐ OWN ☐

I'M FIRED UP!

FYRE
CLUB: OPPOSITES **RARITY:** FABULOUS

WANT ☐ OWN ☐

I ONLY PAINT SELFIES.

UR GETTING V. SLEEPY.

OPTICAL

CLUB: ART **RARITY:** FABULOUS

WANT ☐ OWN ☐

SURREAL BEBÉ

CLUB: ART **RARITY:** FABULOUS

WANT ☐ OWN ☐

CHECK ME!

DON'T WORRY, B.B. HAPPY!

JAMMIN'

CLUB: DANCE **RARITY:** FABULOUS

WANT ☐ OWN ☐

HARLEQUIN GIRL

CLUB: ART **RARITY:** FABULOUS

WANT ☐ OWN ☐

LIGHTS, SHIMMER, LET'S SHINE!

Let's see what show-stoppers 2021 has in store for you.

Tick the five words from the list that really appeal to you.

Then let's see how you'll shine in 2021.

- ◯ energy
- ◯ adventure
- ◯ achievement
- ◯ spotlight
- ◯ champion

- ◯ create
- ◯ daydream
- ◯ imagination
- ◯ doodle
- ◯ freedom

- ◯ understand
- ◯ listen
- ◯ loyalty
- ◯ positivity
- ◯ friendship
- ◯ giggles

ADD UP YOUR TICKS AND LET'S CONSULT THE DESTINY DECODER!

If you ticked mostly...

RED

You're fired up for an action-packed 2021! You know that hard work gets you places, and 2021 is the year you'll go there. So smash that schoolwork, blitz those hobbies, and enjoy your time in the spotlight!

BLUE

2021 is all about expressing yourself through art, fashion and music. You love to create, and you'll inspire others with your amazing ideas and show stopping results. Stock up on those crafting supplies, you're going to need them!

GREEN

Friendship is what it's all about for you and 2021 will be the year you go large on being the best friend anyone could wish for. You'll be focusing on kindness, fun and bringing a dash of goodness to everyone's day. And in return, your friendships will be stronger than ever!

MAKIN' A DIFFERENCE!

Draw lines to match up the opposite words. Can you find the word that doesn't have an opposite?

Harlequin Girl loves to find the opposite in everything.

BIG

DAY

ORDINARY

LEFT

UP

HOT

RELAXED

GLITTER

TOP

BOTTOM

STRESSED

COLD

DOWN

NIGHT

RIGHT

SMALL

EXTRAORDINARY

The word that doesn't have an opposite is _____

ALL MIXT UP

Finish the other half of Harlequin Girl, drawing square by square. When you're done, follow the colour key to get Harlequin's mixed up look picture perfect.

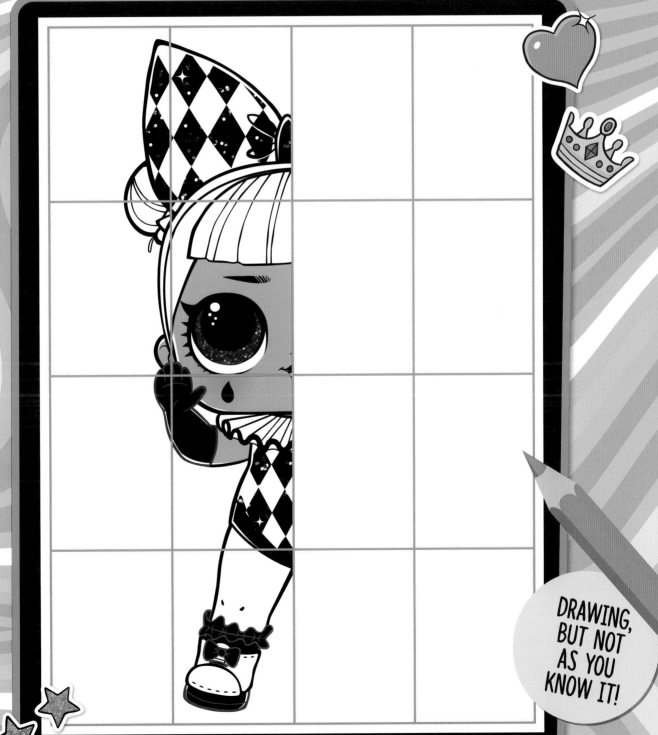

DRAWING, BUT NOT AS YOU KNOW IT!

DRIP DROP'S FASHION REVEAL!

Who's your perfect fashion friend?
Tick an answer for each question, then
reveal your fashion friendship match!

1 WHICH SHOE IS SO TOTALLY YOU?

A   B   C

2 CHOOSE THE TASTIEST FRUIT.

A   B   B

3 WHICH SPORT WOULD BE SO YOU?

A   B   C

© MGA

4 WHAT'S YOUR FAVOURITE WEATHER?

A

B

C

5 CHOOSE A GREAT NIGHT OUT.

A
Walking the catwalk and meeting your biggest fashion fans.

B
Reporting on the latest trends from the front row.

C
Behind the scenes, adding the last minute touches to my amazing creations!

Now add up your answers to reveal your fashion friend for life.

MOSTLY A'S
You're a fashion ball of energy, and you grab every new fashion trend straight off the front row. Your fashion twin is Fyre cos you're both fierce fashion lovers.

MOSTLY B'S
You love scooping up the latest looks, and putting your own twist on the new season's styles. Your design diva friend is Dancebot.

MOSTLY C'S
You're not one to follow the crowd and your look is totally unique - and that's what makes you fashion fabulous! You're just like Surreal Bebé, because you'll mix 'n; match and anything goes!

SO TOTALLY SURREAL

See if you can solve these random puzzlers!

1 REALLY RANDOM

Surreal Bebé loves abstract art! Can you tell who these L.O.L. abstract portraits are?

A

B

C

2 SILLY SPELLER
Circle every third letter to reveal something Surreal Bebé loves.

DHFBNLIUOHGWZXEASRMKS

© MGA

GIGGLE SQUIGGLES

Draw wiggly lines to match the jokes to the correct answers.

1 WHAT DO ELVES LEARN IN SCHOOL?

2 WHY DID THE TEDDY BEAR SAY "NO" TO DESSERT?

A A PALM TREE!

B LOST.

3 WHAT KIND OF TREE FITS IN YOUR HAND?

4 WHAT DO YOU CALL A PENGUIN IN THE DESERT?

C THE ELF-ABET.

D BECAUSE SHE WAS STUFFED.

4

PHOTO FINISH

Which piece is missing from the photograph of Surreal Surreal Bebé and her pals?

Answers on pages 76-77.   © MGA

MUSIC IS MY JAM!

Jammin' can play every musical instrument she can get her hands on.

O	V	S	D	R	A	O	B	Y	E	K	R	O	I	J
L	B	K	C	R	T	L	T	E	B	J	E	N	O	N
E	A	O	N	R	R	Q	R	O	D	C	V	D	A	Z	U
E	F	E	E	T	U	G	X	I	I	G	R	I	H	U
I	N	U	T	M	Z	T	F	T	V	U	O	P	K	K
B	D	O	P	K	T	T	P	R	B	V	C	V	D	E
T	A	E	H	Z	X	J	U	Y	E	P	E	H	V	L
J	T	S	N	P	C	U	T	M	I	M	R	P	N	E
A	D	Q	S	O	O	E	S	B	O	A	U	D	L	L
G	V	I	L	O	N	X	T	R	O	M	B	O	N	E
N	R	L	X	I	O	G	A	N	P	L	V	M	N	K
C	E	I	R	J	D	N	E	S	K	L	D	R	T	G
C	F	A	E	H	T	W	G	G	R	Z	J	Z	N	P
G	L	A	E	G	P	K	J	F	Q	Y	Y	C	M	H
C	R	W	S	N	I	L	O	I	V	D	R	U	M	S

Answers on pages 76-77.

SEE HOW MANY INSTRUMENTS YOU CAN FIND IN THE GRID. CROSS EACH WORD OFF AS YOU FIND IT.

- [ ] Violin
- [ ] Viola
- [ ] Keyboards
- [ ] Piano
- [ ] Cello
- [ ] Recorder
- [ ] Clarinet
- [ ] Oboe
- [ ] Saxophone
- [ ] Drums
- [ ] Bassoon
- [ ] Ukelele
- [ ] Trumpet
- [ ] Trombone

© MGA

DOWN TO A TEE!

Use Jammin's clues to work out which order the t-shirts go in. Draw on each design as you solve the clues.

The lolly design is in between the ice cream and melon designs.

The smiley is below the melon.

The lightning is to the left of the diamond and the smiley.

KEY:

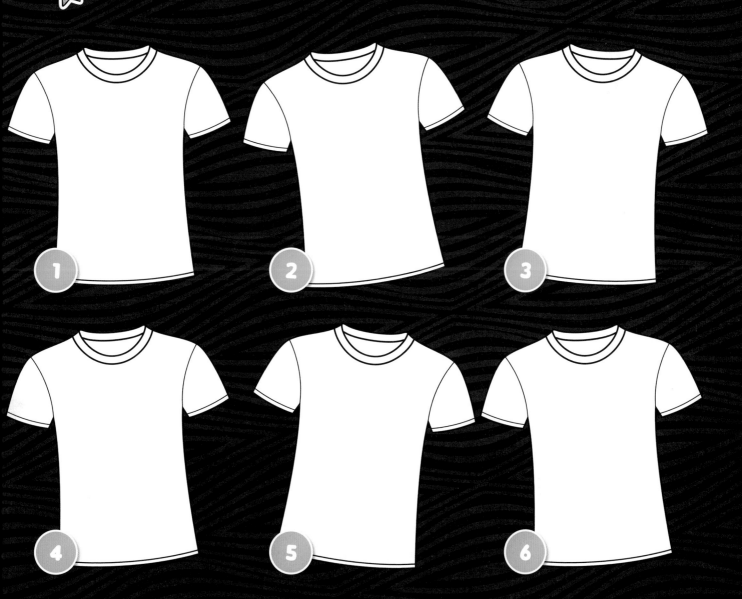

1
2
3
4
5
6

HOW TO TOTALLY AWESOME YOUR LIFE

Takin' tips from friendly faces!

OOPS BABY

There isn't a single person who sails through life without a few cringe moments! The best way to get over those embarrassing moments is to laugh them off! And remember - be kind when your friends are having a cringe day - it could be your turn soon!

OOPS BABY'S TIP: WRITE DOWN ALL YOUR CRINGEY MOMENTS IN A DIARY – YOU'LL LAUGH LOOKING BACK ON THEM.

BE THE BEST YOU

Fierce has a passion for fashion, and that drives her to be her best self every day. What's your passion? Whatever you love in life, push yourself to get better and better until you're the best you can be at the things you love!

FIERCE'S TIP: WHAT DO YOU LIKE TO DO? SPEND SOME TIME RESEARCHING YOUR PASSION AND SEE HOW YOU CAN BE BETTER!

LET IT ALL GO

Metal Babe loves to rock out after a hard day at the forefront of fashion! Being a total fashion diva can be busy and demanding, so she likes to let it all go to her favourite tunes! When you're feeling stressed, turn up the tunes and rock out for all it's worth!

METAL BABE'S TIP: MAKE UP A DISTRESSING DANCE ROUTINE THAT YOU DO EVERY DAY.

© MGA

PLAN, PLAN PLAN

Make like Independent Queen and spend some time to plan your next bold moves! Independent Queen knows exact what she wants and she knows they key to getting it is to have a good plan. She loves ticking things off her to-do list and getting closer to her dreams line-by-line!

INDEPENDENT QUEEN'S TIP: DESIGN A PLANNER WITH A WEEKLY CHECKLIST – GOTTA MAKE THOSE DREAMS A REALITY!

BE THE STAR OF YOUR OWN SHOW

Supa Star's rule is - it's your life, live it the way you want to! She doesn't follow the crowd and stays focused on her goal of becoming a total global superstar! It's great to be part of a fierce friendship crowd, but sometimes you gotta go your own way and focus on yourself!

SUPA STAR'S TIP: TAKE SOME TIME EVERY WEEK AWAY FROM FRIENDS TO CONCENTRATE ON YOUR HOBBIES.

ENJOY!

Luxe likes the good things in life and knows taking time away from the fashion front row leaves her fresh for the next fashion day! Make time to treat yourself, whether that's reading a book, playing in the park or spending time with friends. Don't forget to add a dash of kindness, and most of all, have fun!

LUXE'S TIP: PLAN A PAMPER NIGHT ONCE EVERY WEEK!

© MGA

GOING DOTTY

This puzzle is on fire! Can you work out how many red dots are on the page?

There are _____ red dots.

© MGA

Answers on pages 76-77.

SEEING THINGS

Thinking you've got this? Think again!

Optical loves brain-boggling illusions. See if you have crystal clear vision with these puzzlers.

1 Which line is longer - horizontal or vertical?

2 Which dot is bigger?

Answers on pages 76-77.

SPEAKIN' BODY LANGUAGE

PICK THE DANCE MOVE THAT'S MOST LIKE YOURS.

Find out what your moves say about you.

THE ROBOT

You like to plan your dance moves, and you're a born planner in life, too. You'll practise until you're totally perfect!

ONE HAND IN THE AIR

You're a free spirit and you don't like to worry too much about what others might be thinking. You have creativity running through your bones, and on the dance floor, too.

SHIMMY

You love learning the latest routines on Tik Tok and you always show up to the dance floor with something new. You're like this in life, too, snapping up new trends and trailblazing the latest fashions.

© MGA

CHOREOGRAPHED

You're conscientious and dedicated, whether it's a dance routine or your school work. You hate being bored and you won't start something unless you know you can see it through!

ARMS IN THE AIR

You're an extrovert. You own that dance-floor with your dramatic moves, and don't care who's watching. The more attention you get the better!

OPEN ARMS

You like to do things differently, ripping up the rule book and reinventing things your own way! You're always excited to try new things, and you don't worry too much about what others think.

TURNED IN KNEES

You have a unique way of looking at the world and although you might appear bold and brash, you're an introvert at heart. You don't like being the centre of attention, preferring to let your moves and look speak for itself!

©MGA

NICE 'N' NEON

Time to turn the brightness UP!

Jammin' is never without a pop of bright colour. It lifts her mood and she always stands out from the crowd. Here's how to add a dash of bright to your day.

SPRAY AWAY

Neon hair colours are perfect for when you want to change up your look. Simply choose your shade, spray and you're done! Remember to get wash out spray, so you can have a different colour next time.

ADD A POP OF NEON TO THE HAIR MANNEQUIN.

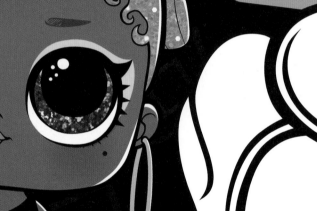

CLASSIC... WITH A TWIST

Jammin' loves to add her own spin to catwalks looks. Her shapes might be classic, but her colours always clash - and they clash good! Take classic prints like leopard print or zebra stripes, and neon them up!

ADD SOME NEON SHADES TO THIS CLASSIC PRINT.

LAYER UP THE ACCESSORIES

Colour popping shades can brighten your mood, but what can you do when it's a school day? Easy. Go large on your accessories! Wear your colours on your pencil case, school bag and lunch box. Seeing a pop of bright colour will always put a smile on your face.

GIVE THESE SCHOOLDAYS ACCESSORIES AN EYE-POPPING MAKEOVER.

MAKE THIS HOODIE AS BRIGHT AS YOU CAN!

WEAR IT PROUD

Bring some colour back to the weekends, by adding some bright colours to your wardrobe. We're talking eye-popping coral tops, lime green hoodies, yellow shorts and multi-coloured accessories. It's your down time, so go for it!

DON'T FORGET A SMILE

Neon colours are all about feeling cheerful and bright, so don't forget to finish your look with a megawatt beam. Looking's bright, feelin' bright!

MEET... THE POP GIRLS

These L.O.L.s are all about the music!

80S B.B.

GET INTO THE GROOVE, B.B.!

CLUB: POP **RARITY:** FANCY

WANT ☐ OWN ☐

OOPS BABY

SOMETIMES I CRAWL, SOMETIMES I CRY.

CLUB: POP **RARITY:** POPULAR

WANT ☐ OWN ☐

SUPA STAR

I WANNA DANCE WITH SOME B.B.

CLUB: GLEE **RARITY:** FANCY

WANT ☐ OWN ☐

© MGA

R U A STAR MATE?

How well do you know UR bestie... really?

#1

THIS QUIZ IS ABOUT ....

1 What's my favourite colour? ....

2 What do I like to eat more than anything? ....

3 What are my hobbies? ....

4 Do like crafts? ....

5 Am I sporty? ....

6 Who is my teacher? ....

7 Who do I admire? ....

8 Which animals do I think are cute? ....

9 Do I have any brothers or sisters? ....

10 What job do I want to do when I'm older? ....

Did you get any
answers wrong? No
worries, this just shows
the areas that you and
your bestie need to
work on to become
total twins!

© MGA

PIN THE BOW ON DIVA

How close can you get it?

Trace Diva's bow

YOU'LL NEED:

Paper
Scissors
Pens
Sticky tack

INSTRUCTIONS

- Carefully trace Diva's bow on to a piece of paper.
- Colour it in.
- Cut it out.
- Attach a blob of sticky tack to the back of the bow.
- Stand this page up, then close your eyes and see if you can stick Diva's bow in the right place!

Requires scissors

ASK A GROWN-UP FOR HELP WITH CUTTING OUT.

29

WILL YOUR NAME BRING YOU FAME?

See what star turn you'll take when you grow up!

INSTRUCTIONS

1 Write your full name on a piece of paper.

2 Underneath each letter, write how many times it appears in the words

EXAMPLE: **AN L.O.L SURPRISE!**
1 1 _ 1 2 _1_ 1 2 1 2 1 = **13** 1+3 = **4**

3 Add up the numbers. If you get a double figure, keep adding the numbers together until you get a single figure.

4 Now find your fame name game on the grid opposite!

© MGA

1

You might feel a little shy sometimes, but being a famous Tik Tok-er would suit you!

2

You're always able to get the audience laughing. You'd be great at comedy.

3

You'd find fame as an environment-loving conservationist.

4

People would travel far and wide to attend one of your crazy energy shows.

5

Creativity is your thing and you'd be best suited as a famous fashion designer.

6

Your art shows will get the whole world talking. Your talent is incredible!

7

Take up an instrument because you'll find fame as part of the band!

8

You'll set the world alight with your amazing advances in science.

9

Have you tried acting? Get some lesson's cos it's so gonna be your thing!

WHAT'S THE SECRET?

80s B.B. is unveiling her latest tune!

80s B.B. is showing off her tune to Goo-Goo Queen. There's a hidden message in it! Use the key to find out what all the letters in bold are saying.

JU**M**P UP AND DA**NC**E
IT'S ALL ABOUT ROMANC**E**
SOME **P**EOPLE SAY I'M SM**O**OTH
BUT I'M JUST GETTING IN THE **G**ROOVE!

The secret message is:

___ ___ ___ ___ ___

___ ___

KEY

M = J
N = U
C = S
E = T

S = D
P = A
O = N
B = C
G = E

TOY

Answers on pages 76-77.

© MGA

TAKIN' IT BACK...
WAY BACK!

Biker boots and ruffled skirts? 80s B.B. is taking it back decades. It's grunge mixed with pretty touches like bows and ruffles.

Design her a new outfit, here:

TOY

L.O.L. Surprise!

33

© MGA

MEET... THE R&B GIRLS

These girls are all about the booming bass line!

KITTY QUEEN

PURR-FECTION

CLUB: GLITTERATI **RARITY:** RARE

WANT ☐ OWN ☐

BEATS

CRAZYSLEEPYCOOL

CLUB: HIP HOP **RARITY:** FANCY

WANT ☐ OWN ☐

IM EXTRA VERY EXTRA

L.O.L SURPRISE

WOO!
we so surprising

INSTAGOLD

LITERALLY CAN'T EVEN.

CLUB: 24K GOLD **RARITY:** ULTRA-RARE

WANT ☐ OWN ☐

LIVE IN CONCERT

KITTY QUEEN

@THE CHOCOLATE BAR

©MGA

FIERCE

DO YOU WANNA BE MY BFF!

CLUB: POP **RARITY:** POPULAR

WANT ☐ OWN ☐

JAMMIN'

DON'T WORRY, B.B. HAPPY.

CLUB: DANCE **RARITY:** FABULOUS

WANT ☐ OWN ☐

DREAMIN' IN DOODLES

Create a musical interlude with Oops Baby.

Scribble and colour a scene for Oops Baby.

IN THE BAG!

L.O.L. girls don't leave home without all their essentials!

Look at Oops Baby's bag for 20 seconds. Cool isn't it! But REALLY look, because we want you to turn the page and draw it all again. Easy? **LET'S SEE!**

WHAT'S IN OOPS BABY'S PURSE?

Let's put your drawing skills to the test!

#1

Did you look at the picture on the previous page? Good! Now it's time to see how much you remember! See if you can draw the purse and all the items in it. Flick back a page to see how you did.

© MGA

HITTIN' THE SPOT!

Only pizza hits the spot after a night spittin' rhymes!

The girls are hungry after a gig. Which is the missing piece of pizza? M.C.N.Y.C. has ordered pizzas for the hip hop crew. Draw lines to match the correct slices to the pizzas!

A

B

C

D

1
2

3
4

Answers on pages 76-77.

© MGA

39

MAKE SURPRISE SWEETIE CUPCAKES

Delicious… with a difference! Hops loves to make these L.O.L. cupcakes packed with a cute surprise.

DOES RUNNING LATE COUNT AS EXERCISE?

INGREDIENTS

100g margarine or butter

100g caster sugar

2 eggs

1/2 teaspoon vanilla extract

100g self-raising flour

Smarties or other sweets

Can of icing

Sprinkles, edible glitter (optional)

METHOD:

1. Preheat the oven to 200°C / Gas 6.

2. Mix the butter and sugar together until fluffy.

3. Add eggs and vanilla essence, and fold together until you have smooth mixture.

4. Fold in the flour and mix well.

5. Transfer the mix to the cupcake cases.

6. Bake for 15 minutes.

FOR THE SURPRISE:

1. Once the cupcakes are cool, carefully cut a hole in the middle of each one.

2. Fill the hole with smarties, or your chosen sweet.

FOR THE ICING:

1. Take your icing can, and carefully swirl across the top of the cupcake, making sure to cover up your sweetie surprise!

2. Add finishing touches with sprinkles or edible glitter!

3. Allow to cool, decorate as desired and serve.

PURPLE REIGN

Royalty is in the house!

THROWIN' SHADE

Which shadow matches Purple Queen?

A B C D E

FAMILY PORTRAITS

Can you tell who this queen is?

PURPLE QUEEN

OOPS BABY

80S B.B.

LET'S GET LOST

Lead Purple Queen through the maze to Oops Baby.

START

FINISH

GOO-GOO QUEEN

OUT OF TIME

Which Superstar is the odd one out?

A

B

C

D

E

SUPA STAR

MEET... THE HIP HOP GIRLS

These girls always know how to mix it up.

HONEY BUN

ALL YOU BABY MC'S AIN'T GOT NOTHIN' ON ME!

CLUB: HIP HOP **RARITY:** POPULAR

WANT ☐ OWN ☐

M.C.N.Y.C.

CHECK IT!

CLUB: RETRO **RARITY:** POPULAR

WANT ☐ OWN ☐

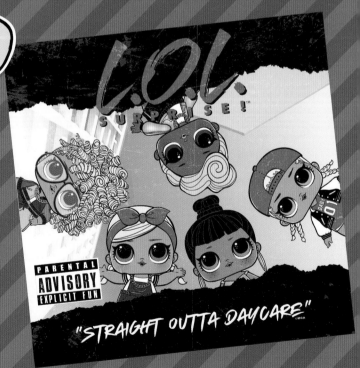

L.O.L. SURPRISE!

PARENTAL ADVISORY EXPLICIT FUN

"STRAIGHT OUTTA DAYCARE"

© MGA

D.J.

LITERALLY CAN'T EVEN.

CLUB: HIP HOP **RARITY:** FANCY

WANT ☐ OWN ☐

M.C. SWAG

STRAIGHT OUTTA DAYCARE.

BABY 01

CLUB: GLEE **RARITY:** POPULAR

WANT ☐ OWN ☐

SHORTY

SHORTY-LICIOUS FOR YA, BABE!

CLUB: HIP HOP **RARITY:** POPULAR

WANT ☐ OWN ☐

A-Z OF L.O.L.S

Learning all about these gals is easy as a, b, c!

A IS FOR AWESOME.
Get ready to act like the star you are!

B IS FOR BABIES.
They run the world y'know!

C IS FOR CONFIDENCE.
Believe in yourself and always be nice to others.

D IS FOR DANCING.
Don't ever stop, it makes you feel brilliant.

E IS FOR EXTRA.
The L.O.L. crew always know how to bring it.

F IS FOR FIERCE, FAST AND FEARLESS.
The only way to live.

G IS FOR GIGGLES.
Friends who giggle together, stay together. It's official.

H IS FOR HUGGING.
Everyone needs a good ol' squeeze from time to time.

I IS FOR IMAGINATION.
Dream big, cos the sky really is the limit.

J IS FOR JUST DOING YOUR THING.
You don't have to go with the flow.

K IS FOR KINDNESS.
It's cool to be kind, y'know.

L IS FOR LIMELIGHT.
There's nothing wrong with stealing it every so often!

M IS FOR MAGICAL.
These dolls certainly know how to work their magic!

N IS FOR NAPPING.
A girl's gotta get her beauty sleep.

O IS FOR OUTFITS.
You can never have too many.

P IS FOR POSITIVE VIBES.
Add some instant happy sass to your life.

46

© MGA

Q
IS FOR
QUEEN!
Be the queen of your own life. Yaaaaas!

R
IS FOR
ROCKIN' OUT
L.O.L. gals could rock before they could walk.

S
IS FOR
SHINING BRIGHT LIKE A DIAMOND.
Smile at everyone, it's totally contagious.

T
IS FOR
TEAM PLAYER.
Everyone will love you for it!

U
IS FOR
ULTIMATE DREAM!
The L.O.L. dolls are livin it now, and you could too.

V
IS FOR
VICTORIOUS.
Go after what you want and make sure you get it!

W
IS FOR
WELCOMING.
Go outta your way to make others feel comfy.

X
IS FOR
X FACTOR.
You've got it, so work it and own it, girlfriend.

Y
IS FOR
YAAAAAAS!
Life's too short for anything else!

Z
IS FOR
ZZZ'S.
Being a L.O.L. gal is exhausting, but so much fun!

ALL YOU BABY MC'S AIN'T GOT NOTHIN' ON ME!

GET THE LOOK!

Rockin' M.C.N.Y.C.'s style couldn't be easier.

YOU GOT THIS!

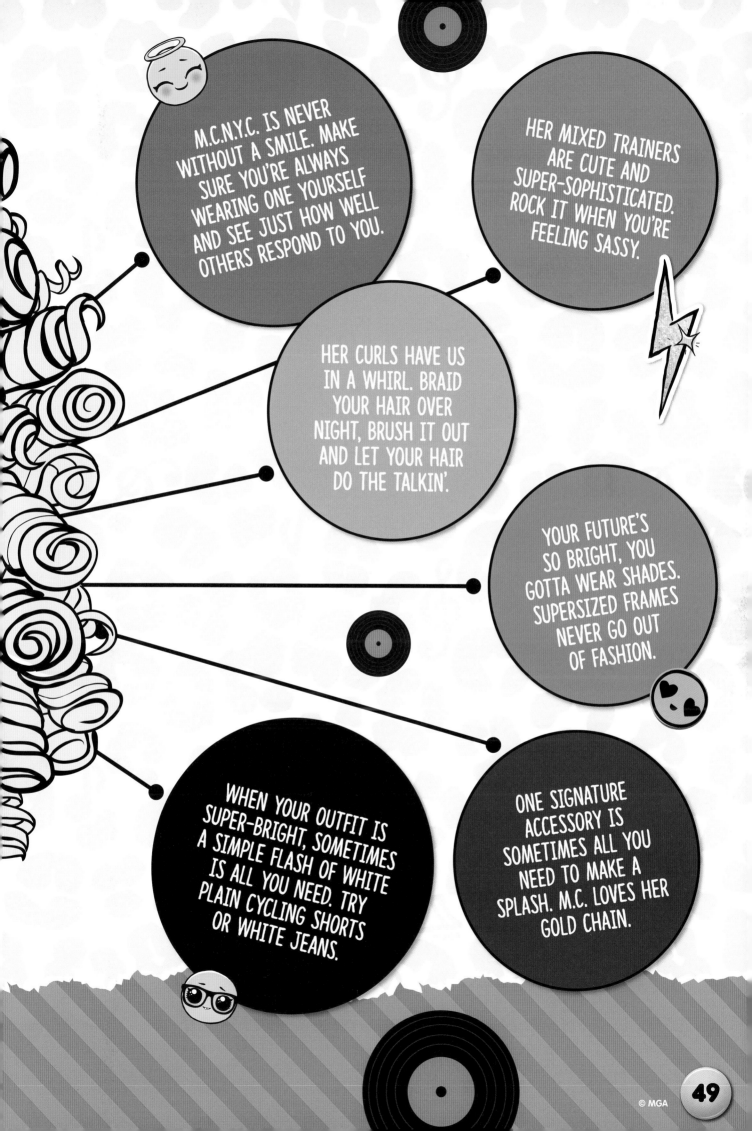

M.C.N.Y.C. IS NEVER WITHOUT A SMILE. MAKE SURE YOU'RE ALWAYS WEARING ONE YOURSELF AND SEE JUST HOW WELL OTHERS RESPOND TO YOU.

HER MIXED TRAINERS ARE CUTE AND SUPER-SOPHISTICATED. ROCK IT WHEN YOU'RE FEELING SASSY.

HER CURLS HAVE US IN A WHIRL. BRAID YOUR HAIR OVER NIGHT, BRUSH IT OUT AND LET YOUR HAIR DO THE TALKIN'.

YOUR FUTURE'S SO BRIGHT, YOU GOTTA WEAR SHADES. SUPERSIZED FRAMES NEVER GO OUT OF FASHION.

WHEN YOUR OUTFIT IS SUPER-BRIGHT, SOMETIMES A SIMPLE FLASH OF WHITE IS ALL YOU NEED. TRY PLAIN CYCLING SHORTS OR WHITE JEANS.

ONE SIGNATURE ACCESSORY IS SOMETIMES ALL YOU NEED TO MAKE A SPLASH. M.C. LOVES HER GOLD CHAIN.

♪ IN A SPIN ♪

Help the Hip Hop crew solves these mind-bending puzzles!

VINYL MIX-UP

Draw a circle around the record that is connected to the deck so M.C. Swag knows what to play next.

A

B

C

MIRROR MESSAGE

D.J. has left you a message in a nightclub mirror. Can you work out what it says?

ALWAYS
READY FOR
MY SELFIE!

- [ ] **Rizzle**
- [ ] **Fo'shizzle**
- [ ] **Fly**
- [ ] **Kicks**
- [ ] **Chill**
- [ ] **Da bomb**
- [ ] **Word**
- [ ] **What up**

TICK THEM OFF AS YOU FIND THEM.

LINGO SEARCH

The Hip Hop crew have their own lingo. Hop to it and find all the words hidden in the grid.

F	K	E	I	B	Y	C	K	L	I	N	M	N	M	H
B	O	Q	X	Z	H	B	J	R	E	T	N	S	S	J
X	W	S	R	Q	S	B	S	F	S	B	L	E	Z	F
K	F	D	H	Y	P	K	O	M	C	X	R	H	I	R
N	S	T	T	I	Q	R	C	A	M	Y	I	M	F	L
N	I	O	Y	P	Z	T	P	I	B	Y	D	R	P	L
K	P	V	R	V	N	Z	P	A	K	C	E	Q	X	I
I	W	U	J	Q	D	A	L	B	R	L	Y	X	I	H
Y	P	U	T	A	H	W	W	E	I	F	L	Y	I	C
X	F	G	B	M	M	M	S	N	Z	K	B	K	D	T
B	Z	O	B	S	R	B	M	X	Z	C	V	R	X	H
F	M	E	B	O	G	R	C	F	L	M	O	S	W	G
B	H	P	S	T	G	V	A	B	E	W	Q	C	P	V
E	W	S	X	X	E	X	P	J	E	P	G	G	L	M
Y	U	I	L	M	A	E	M	V	U	T	K	K	G	W

Answers on pages 76-77.

SHORTY-LICIOUS BINGO

Every time these L.O.L. Surprise!-based things happen, tick it off your playing card. That's bingo-vicious for you!

HOW TO PLAY

1. Grab a friend (or play on your own), and tick off the things that you spot.
2. When you spot them, you must accept the L.O.L. Surprise! challenge!

SOMEONE TAKING A SELFIE

Take a selfie of the silliest expression you can pull.

SOMEONE LAUGHING

Tell the next person you see your favourite joke. (Whether or not they want to hear it.).

SOMEONE WEARING SUNGLASSES

Find your fave photo of you and your BFFs and put it in a frame next to your bed.

A CAT

Make up a dance routine and teach it to your dad/uncle/next-door-neighbour.

SOMEONE DANCING

Shout, "I love L.O.L. Surprise!" out of the nearest window.

SOMETHING WITH GLITTER ON

For the next hour you can only communicate through the language of dance.

SOMEONE WEARING BLING ACCESSORIES

The next time someone speaks to you, you can only repeat what they say.

SOMEONE WEARING SNEAKERS

Do 20 star jumps as fast as you can.

SOMEONE TAKING A SELFIE

Give yourself a hair makeover. Make it fierce!

BRING THE NOISE

Copy this picture of the Hip Hops BFFs into the large grid.

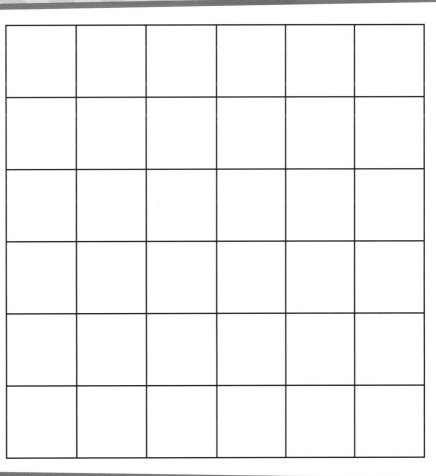

© MGA

MEET... THE GLAM ROCK/ PUNK GANG

Feel the noize!
These fashionistas are the
coolest crew in town.

THE QUEEN

I'M ALL SHOOK UP!

CLUB: GLITTERATI **RARITY:** RARE

WANT ☐ OWN ☐

METAL BABE

ROCK ON!

CLUB: OPPOSITES **RARITY:** POPULAR

WANT ☐ OWN ☐

For the record
Off the record

I'm extra,
Very extra

GRUNGE
GRRRL

I got mad Swag

54 © MGA

GRUNGE GRRRL

LET'S RIOT!

CLUB: ROCK **RARITY:** POPULAR

WANT ☐ OWN ☐

NEVER MIND
THE OTHER TOYS
HERE'S

L.O.L.
SuRPRise!

PUNK BOI

OFF THE RECORD

REBEL AGAINST NAPTIME!

CLUB: ROCK **RARITY:** ULTRA-RARE

WANT ☐ OWN ☐

SAY IT PROUD!

Get ready to rock on. Choose one of the Glam Rock sayings to reveal what kind of superstar you are!

Tick the below statement that speaks the most to your inner rocker!

- ☐ **REBEL AGAINST NAPTIME!**
- ☐ **ROCK ON!**
- ☐ **LET'S RIOT!**
- ☐ **I'M ALL SHOOK UP!**

NOW READ ON TO FIND OUT WHAT YOUR CHOICE REVEALS ABOUT YOU, ROCK STAR!

REBEL AGAINST NAPTIME!

You want to show the world what a superstar you are. You want to make sure the whole world knows your name.

LET'S RIOT!

Everybody knows who you are. You're determined to make your dreams come true. You never sit back and wait for things to happen.

ROCK ON!

You want everyone to know the real you, and never ever put on an act. You won't go changing for anyone or anything.

I'M ALL SHOOK UP!

You're down to earth, but you're still one of a kind, and you want everyone to recognise it. You'll always be true to yourself though.

© MGA

TOTALLY MAJESTIC

Draw a fierce self-portrait that's fit for a Queen.

© MGA

BFFS ROCK!

Thrash out your friendship rules with Metal Babe.

MAKE FRIENDS FAST

Making new friends can be so scary, it's hairy. Nail these top tips and you'll have BFFs by the bucket-load.

1. Don't be scared of starting a chat. Ask lots of questions to keep the convo' flowing.

2. Act confident, easy and breezy (even if you don't feel like it at first) and people will flock to be with you!

3. Take up a new hobby. You'll meet loads of new people and can bond over doing something new.

4. Be positive! Make sure your whole vibe is upbeat. No one wants to hang out with a Moaning Minnnie, girlfriend.

KEEP THEM FOREVER!

Once you've made fab BFFs, don't let your friendships slide. Try these pro tips and you'll have pals for life.

1. Laugh out loud. Giggles are free and they make you and your buddies feel good.

2. It's all about trust. Let your friends know you'll be there for them, no matter what!

3. Have you ever had that horrible feeling of being left out? Make sure this never happens to your mates, by inviting them to everything.

4. Spot the signs when something is wrong. If you notice when your mates aren't feeling great, you can fix it fast and put a smile back on her face.

TICK OFF EACH ACTIVITY WHEN YOU COMPLETE IT!

7 DAYS TO BFF PERFECTION

MONDAY	Show love for everyone.	☐
TUESDAY	Ask a favour of someone.	☐
WEDNESDAY	Do something nice for someone new.	☐
THURSDAY	Organise a Zoom catch-up.	☐
FRIDAY	Arrange a dance challenge and invite someone new.	☐
SATURDAY	Go somewhere you've never been before.	☐
SUNDAY	Call someone you know but don't keep in touch with.	☐

©MGA

ASK A GROWN-UP FOR HELP WITH CUTTING OUT.

MINI BFF

Cut out this Metal Babe pencil topper and you'll have a BFF wherever you go.

Cut out your pencil topper. Stick or glue the tabs together around your pencil. Ta da! The most glam pencil in town!

Read page 60 before cutting out the template, or scan this page and print it out.

SUPER SQUARE

The Glam Rockers are many things but they're never square. How many squares can you find in this pattern?

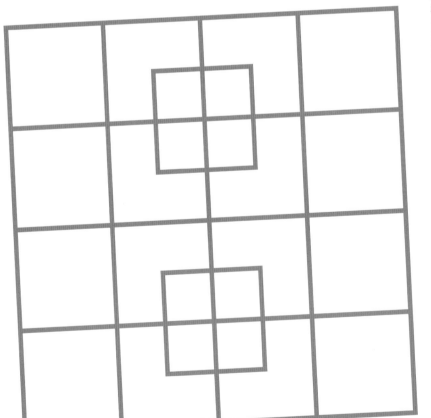

There are _____ squares.

MISCHIEF MAKER

Punk Boi loves getting up to mischief and has set you a brain-tingling puzzle.

#1

Cross out all the letters of the riddle below that appear in the grid, then rearrange the letters left behind to find the answer.

WHAT BELONGS TO YOU, BUT OTHERS USE IT MORE THAN YOU?

S	T	R	E	S	R	G
O	W	Y	U	O	T	H
E	S	O	Y	Y	O	E
N	O	U	H	N	U	O
I	H	A	M	R	E	N
A	A	B	T	M	B	T
T	U	U	L	T	E	O

TROUBLE

__ __ __ __ __ __

__ __ __ __ __

MEET... THE COUNTRY GIRLS

These dolls are a little bit country and always a little bit extra!

LINE DANCER

OH HAY!

CLUB: DANCE **RARITY:** POPULAR

WANT ☐ OWN ☐

TWANG

COWBOY BOOTS GO WITH EVERYTHING!

CLUB: OPPOSITES **RARITY:** POPULAR

WANT ☐ OWN ☐

INDEPENDENT QUEEN

LINE DANCER

LUXE

TWANG

★ L.O.L. SURPRISE! ★

© MGA

INDEPENDENT QUEEN

STARS. STRIPES. SPARKLES. SASS!

CLUB: GLITTERATI **RARITY:** RARE

WANT ☐ OWN ☐

WITH (MY) CREW

COUNTRY STAR

CHERRY

THAT'S WILD!

CLUB: RETRO **RARITY:** POPULAR

WANT ☐ OWN ☐

LUXE

I'VE GOT A HEART OF GOLD.

CLUB: 24K GOLD **RARITY:** ULTRA-RARE

WANT ☐ OWN ☐

DANCE OFF!

Who will win? Only one way to find out, grab your BFFs and start playing...

Read page 66 before cutting out the counters, or scan this page and print it out.

START

1

2

3

4
Spill. Which is your favourite Remix Country L.O.L. doll and why?

16

15

14
The country girls have forgotten their line dance routine. Make one up now.

13

17

18
Draw one of the Country Remix dolls here.

19

20
Put your hair into bunches as fast as you can.

If your pals guess who it is, move forward three spaces.

THE RULES

You need 2-4 players, a coin, drawing materials and some hair bands.

Choose your counters.

The player with the closest birthday to today's date goes first.

Flip a coin to see how many spaces to move: 2 for heads, 1 for tails.

Complete the action on a space to move an extra space.

Whoever gets to the end first, is the winner.

ASK A GROWN-UP FOR HELP WITH CUTTING OUT.

5

6

7

8

Draw a country dance outfit here.

12

11

Do the dosey-doe

10

9

1

22

23

Colour in this cowboy hat now.

24

FINISH

You are the winner! YEE-HA!

COUNTRY STYLE

PONYTAIL

You're a girly-girl who loves clothes, make-up and nails. You love to look neat whatever you're up to. And you wouldn't dream of going out looking anything less than perfect.

Pick your favourite bit of Twang's outfit and see what it reveals about your style.

SHADES

You're quite arty and love experimenting with wild new looks. You hate following the crowds preferring to stand out and turn heads. Go, girl!

CHECKED SHIRT

Beauty treats are low on your list. Life's too short to be stuck in your room painting your nails. You'd rather be out having fun. Yeah, baby!

SHORTS

You know everyone can be stylish. It's not about bold statements or expensive fashions; it's about being creative and knowing what looks good.

COWBOY BOOTS

You'd never wear anything you don't feel comfy in. If you don't feel good, you won't look good. Simples. A fashion rule to definitely live by.

© MGA

ASK ANYTHING!

What would the L.O.L. Surprise! dolls do? Find out here.

HOW TO PLAY

1. Close your eyes and let your hand hover over the below questions.
2. Count to three, then place your index finger on the page.
3. Open your eyes - the question closest to your finger is the question you should ask.

WILL MY DREAMS COME TRUE?

SHOULD I GIVE MYSELF A MAKEOVER?

HOW ABOUT PAINTING MY TOE NAILS THE BRIGHTEST COLOUR I CAN FIND?

IS IT TIME TO TRY OUT A NEW HAIRSTYLE?

SHOULD I TRY SOMETHING NEW TODAY?

© MGA

Now turn over the page, to find out how the L.O.L. Surprise! dolls answer your question.

HOW TO PLAY
Read the answer that is on the back of the question you picked to find out your answer - L.O.L. style!

I DOUBLE DARE YOU!

ASK ME AGAIN LATER!

GO FOR IT!

RIGHT NOW, I'D HAVE TO SAY NO!

ASK YOUR BFF!

WILD SUDOKU

Ready, cowgirls? Fill in the grid with these four parts of Cherry's outfit. Each row, column and four-square block must contain **ONE OF EACH**.

SNEAKER　**SKIRT**　**NECKTIE**　**BOW**

STAR CROSSED

Luxe needs your help solving these bling-tastic puzzles.

WHO'S WHO?

Which of Luxe's friends is hiding behind each star below?

1

2

3

4

STUCK?
USE PAGE 62
TO HELP YOU!

Write out the letters Luxe passes to find out where she's going.

c
n
d
a
i
n
w
F
g
i
t
h
B
F
s

_ _ _ _ _ _ _ _ _ _

_ _ _ _ _ _ _

SHINE ON!

Oops. One of the letters in Luxe's message below has been blinged out. Work out which letter so you can read L.O.L's message.

ALWAYS B☆ FI☆RC☆

BUT WITH A H☆ART

OF GOLD. WORK IT B.B.

ALL MY LOV☆

Luxe xxx

COUNTRY STAR!

Get your creative on and write a country song that's bound to be a No.1. hit!

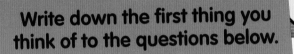

Write down the first thing you think of to the questions below.

1. Your BFF's name

   ....

2. Your BFF's favourite colour (apart from gold)

   ....

3. A word to describe your BFF's popularity

   ....

4. Something you and your BFF do together.

   ....

5. Another word for BFF.

   ....

6. A word that describes your BFF

   ....

We Run the World

© MGA

Now insert your answer into the
numbered gaps to come up with the
song of the century!

A SONG FOR [1] ....

[1] .... This song is all about

Cos they're a super star

Whether dressed in gold or
[2] ....

I always knew they'd go far.

[3] and so full of LOLs .... They're sassy,

I want to let them know they're #friendship goals

[1] for being my friend .... Thank you,

[4] Til the very end .... I know we're gonna

[5] This is for you .... So my dearest

[6] whatever you do! .... Keep on being

SOLO SONGSTER

Just like Twang, you have a passion for music that you can't hide. You'd be incredible on stage belting out the latest song that you've written.

MASTER M.C.

Whether you're making playlists, flicking through vinyls or watching videos on YouTube, you adore music. It's time to start practising your D.J. set, like Luxe.

DANCE TROUPE DARLING

Dancing is definitely your talent, just like Line Dancer. You'd rock in a dance troupe with the other Remix Country girls. Ask your BFFs to give it a try.

ANSWERS

Page 10

Top-bottom, big - small, day - night, hot - cold, left - right, up - down, ordinary - extraordinary, relaxed - stressed.

The word that doesn't have an opposite is glitter.

Pages 14-15

1) A = Optical, B = Fyre, C = DripDrop
2) FLOWERS
3) 1 = C, 2 = D, 3 = A, 4 = B
4) The missing piece is E.

Page 16

O	V	S	D	R	A	O	B	Y	E	K	R	O	I	J
L	B	K	C	R	I	L	T	E	B	J	E	N	O	N
E	A	O	N	R	Q	R	O	D	C	V	D	A	Z	U
E	F	E	E	T	U	G	X	I	I	G	R	I	H	U
I	N	U	T	M	Z	T	F	T	V	U	O	P	K	K
B	D	O	P	K	T	T	P	R	B	V	C	V	D	E
T	A	E	H	Z	X	J	U	Y	E	P	E	H	V	L
J	T	S	N	P	C	U	T	M	I	M	R	P	N	E
A	D	Q	S	O	O	E	S	B	O	A	U	D	L	L
G	V	I	L	O	N	X	T	R	O	M	B	O	N	E
N	R	L	X	I	O	G	A	N	P	L	V	M	N	K
C	E	I	R	J	D	N	E	S	K	L	D	R	T	G
C	F	A	E	H	T	W	G	G	R	Z	J	Z	N	P
G	L	A	E	G	P	K	J	F	Q	Y	Y	C	M	H
C	R	W	S	N	I	L	O	I	V	D	R	U	M	S

Page 17

1) Ice cream. 2) Lolly. 3) Melon
4) Lightning. 5) Diamond. 6) Smiley

Page 20

There are 21 red dots.

Page 21

1) They are the same.
2) The dots are both the same size.

Page 39

A = 1, B = 4, C = 3, D = 2

Pages 42-42

THROWIN' SHADE: E

FAMILY PORTRAITS: Goo-Goo Queen

LET'S GET LOST:

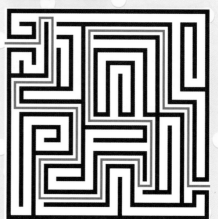

OUT OF TIME: D

Pages 50-51

VINYL MIX-UP: C

MIRROR MESSAGE: Always ready for my selfie!

LINGO SEARCH:

F	K	E	I	B	Y	C	K	L	I	N	M	N	M	H
B	O	O	X	Z	H	B	J	R	E	T	N	S	S	J
X	W	S	R	Q	S	R	S	F	S	B	L	E	Z	F
K	F	D	H	Y	P	K	O	M	C	X	R	H	I	R
N	S	T	T	I	Q	R	C	A	M	Y	I	M	F	L
N	I	O	Y	P	Z	T	P	I	B	Y	D	R	P	L
K	P	V	R	V	N	Z	P	A	K	C	E	Q	X	I
I	W	U	J	Q	D	A	L	B	R	L	Y	X	I	H
Y	P	U	T	A	H	W	W	E	I	F	L	Y	I	C
X	F	G	M	T	N	S	N	Z	K	B	K	D	H	H
B	Z	O	B	S	R	B	M	X	Z	C	Y	R	X	H
F	M	E	B	O	G	R	C	F	L	M	O	S	W	G
B	H	P	S	T	G	V	A	B	E	W	Q	C	P	V
E	W	S	X	X	E	X	P	J	E	P	G	G	L	M
Y	U	I	L	M	A	E	M	V	U	T	K	K	G	W

Page 60

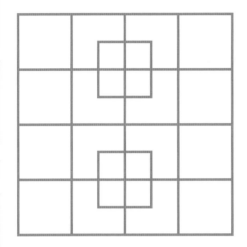

8 tiny squares, 18 single squares, nine 2 x 2 squares, four 3 x 3 squares, and one 4 x 4 square. TOTAL = 40 squares

Page 61

Your name.

Page 69

Page 70

WHO'S WHO?: 1 = Twang, 2 = Cherry, 3 = Independant Queen, 4 = Line Dancer

WHERE U AT?: Dancing with BFF's

SHINE ON!: The missing letter is E.

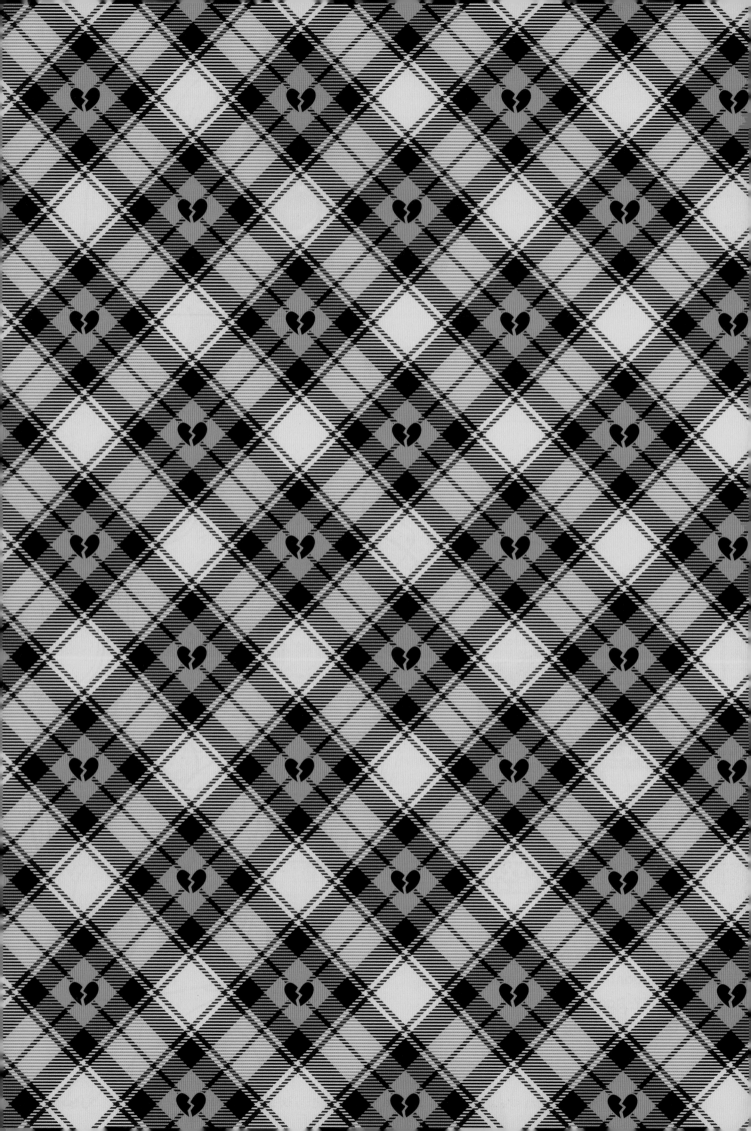